R

Richmond upon Thames Libraries

Renew online at www.richmond.gov.uk/libraries

 LONDON BOROUGH OF
RICHMOND UPON THAMES

D1355315

90710 000 382 518

Inside Animals

Fish

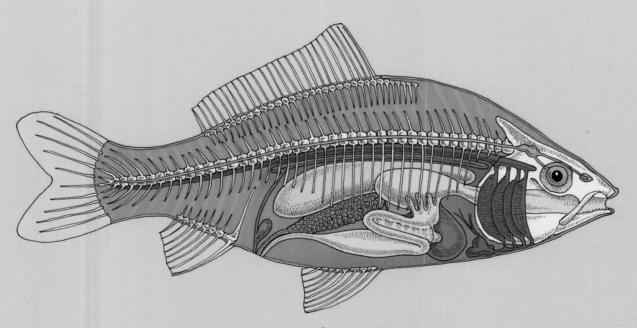

David West

WAYLAND

Wayland
First published in Great Britain in 2018 by Hodder and Stoughton

Copyright © 2018 David West Children's Books

All rights reserved.

Designed and illustrated by David West

HB ISBN 978 1 5263 1085 9
PB ISBN 978 1 5263 1086 6

Printed in Malaysia

Wayland
An imprint of
Hachette Children's Group
Carmelite House
50 Victoria Embankment
London EC4Y 0DZ

An Hachette UK Company
www.hachette.co.uk

www.wayland.co.uk

INSIDE ANIMALS FISH
was produced for Wayland by
David West  Children's Books, 11 Glebe Road, London SW13 0DR

London Borough of Richmond Upon Thames		
RTR	DISCARDED	
90710 000 382 518		
Askews & Holts		
J571.317 WES JUNIOR N	£11.99	
	9781526310859	

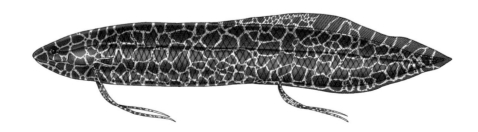

FSC
www.fsc.org

MIX
Paper from
responsible sources
FSC® C010875

Contents

Ray-finned fish — 4

Inside a Ray-finned fish — 6

Shark — 8

Inside a Shark — 10

Seahorse — 12

Inside a Seahorse — 14

Lamprey — 16

Inside a Lamprey — 18

Lungfish — 20

Inside a Lungfish — 22

Glossary and Index — 24

Ray-finned fish

Most fish are ray-finned fish. They are called this because their fins are made of skin stretched over a ray of bones. They are members of the family of fish that has a bony skeleton. Most ray-finned fish are covered in **scales**. They are cold-blooded and the females lay eggs.

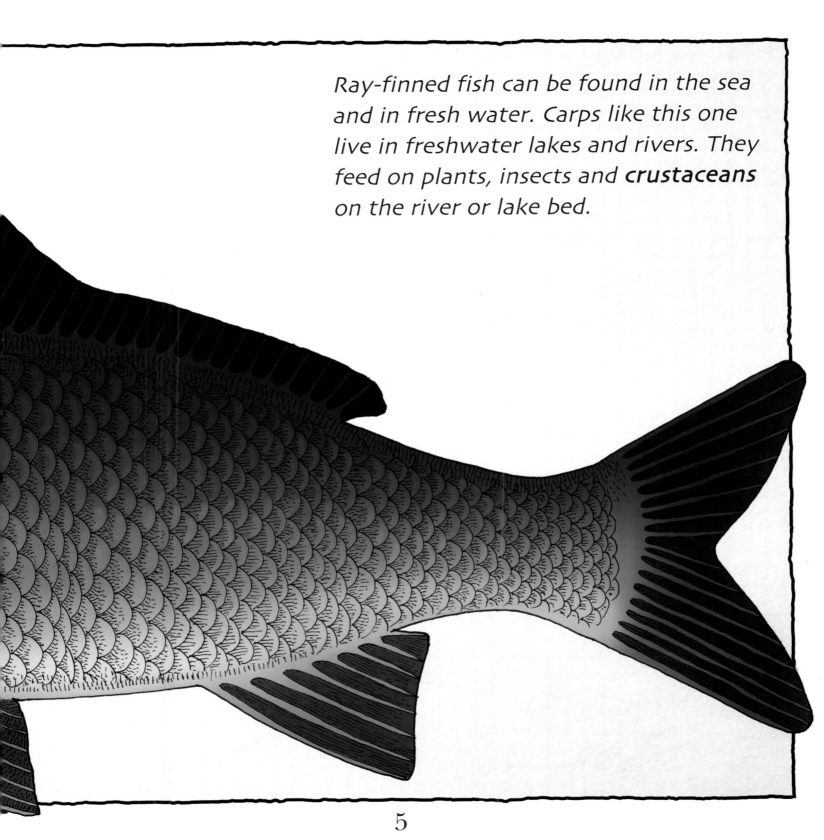

Ray-finned fish can be found in the sea and in fresh water. Carps like this one live in freshwater lakes and rivers. They feed on plants, insects and **crustaceans** on the river or lake bed.

Inside a Ray-finned fish

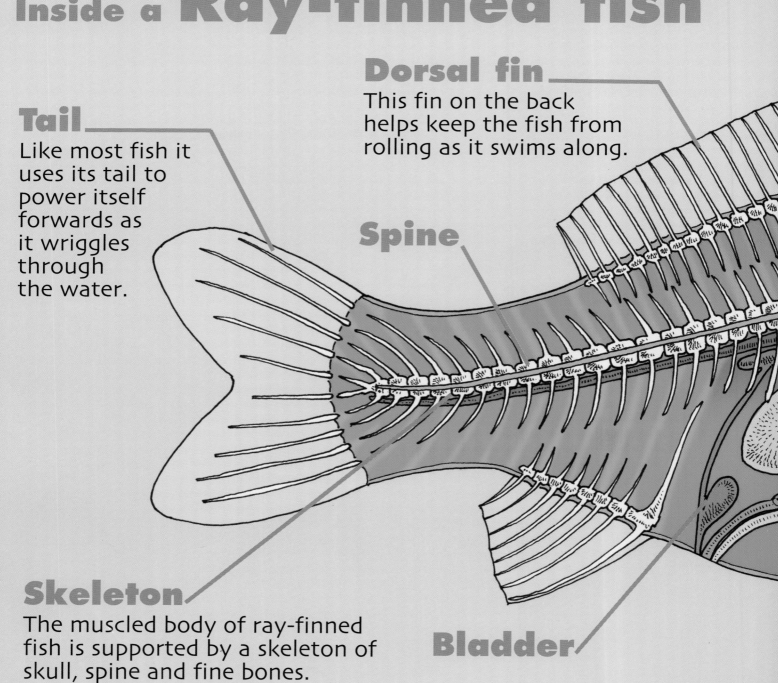

Dorsal fin
This fin on the back helps keep the fish from rolling as it swims along.

Tail
Like most fish it uses its tail to power itself forwards as it wriggles through the water.

Spine

Skeleton
The muscled body of ray-finned fish is supported by a skeleton of skull, spine and fine bones.

Bladder

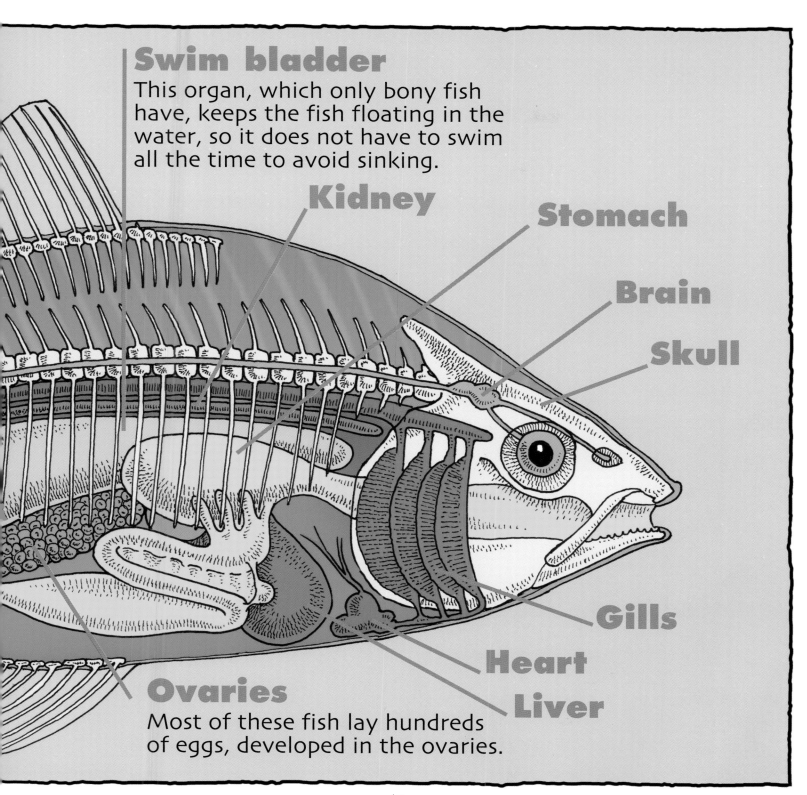

Swim bladder
This organ, which only bony fish have, keeps the fish floating in the water, so it does not have to swim all the time to avoid sinking.

Kidney

Stomach

Brain

Skull

Gills

Heart

Liver

Ovaries
Most of these fish lay hundreds of eggs, developed in the ovaries.

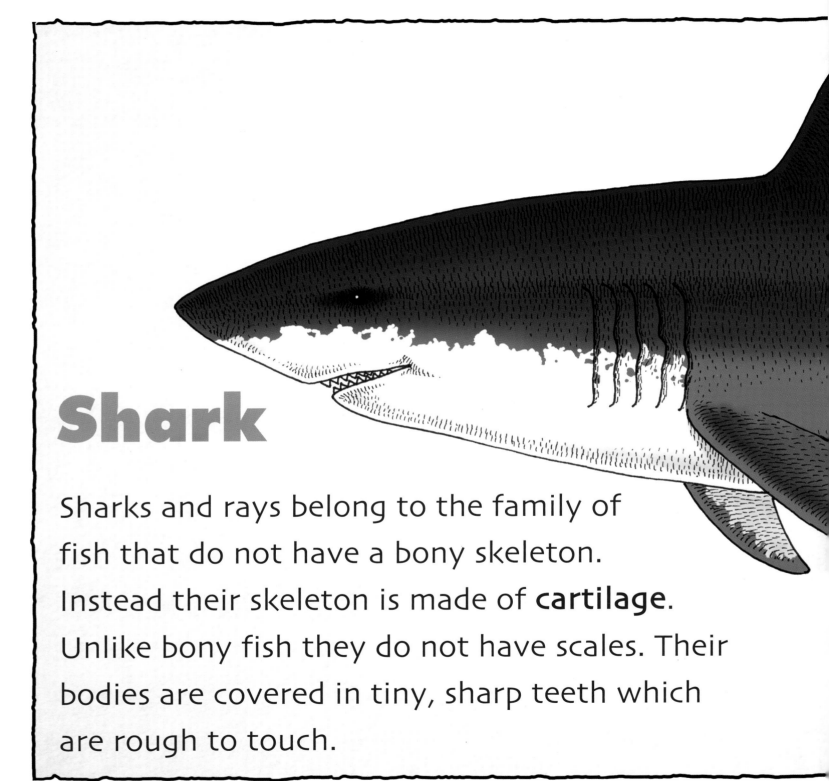

Shark

Sharks and rays belong to the family of
fish that do not have a bony skeleton.
Instead their skeleton is made of **cartilage**.
Unlike bony fish they do not have scales. Their
bodies are covered in tiny, sharp teeth which
are rough to touch.

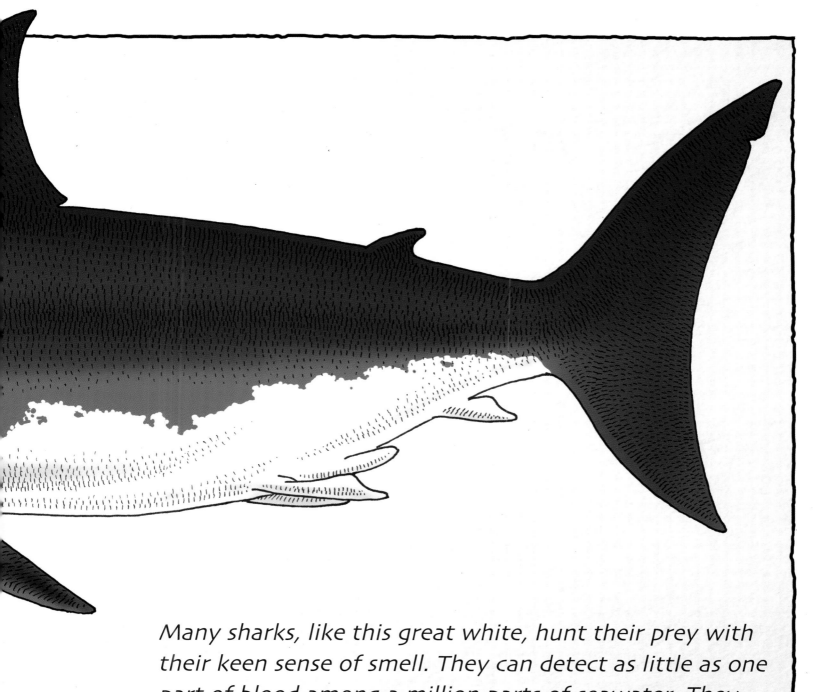

Many sharks, like this great white, hunt their prey with their keen sense of smell. They can detect as little as one part of blood among a million parts of seawater. They also have excellent hearing and have special electrical sensors that can detect prey in murky water.

Inside a **Shark**

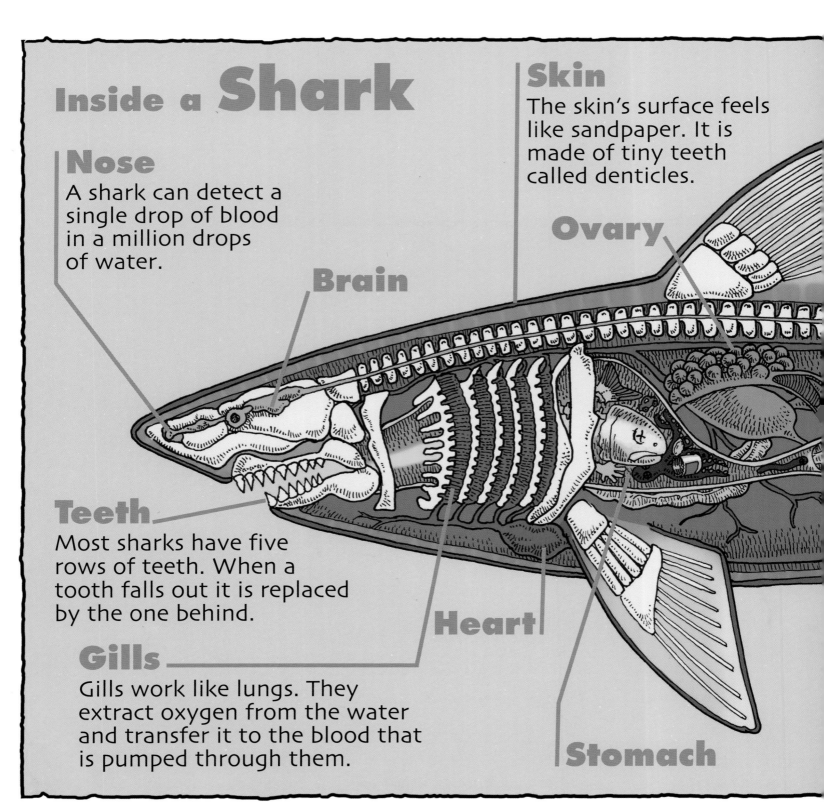

Nose
A shark can detect a single drop of blood in a million drops of water.

Skin
The skin's surface feels like sandpaper. It is made of tiny teeth called denticles.

Ovary

Brain

Teeth
Most sharks have five rows of teeth. When a tooth falls out it is replaced by the one behind.

Heart

Gills
Gills work like lungs. They extract oxygen from the water and transfer it to the blood that is pumped through them.

Stomach

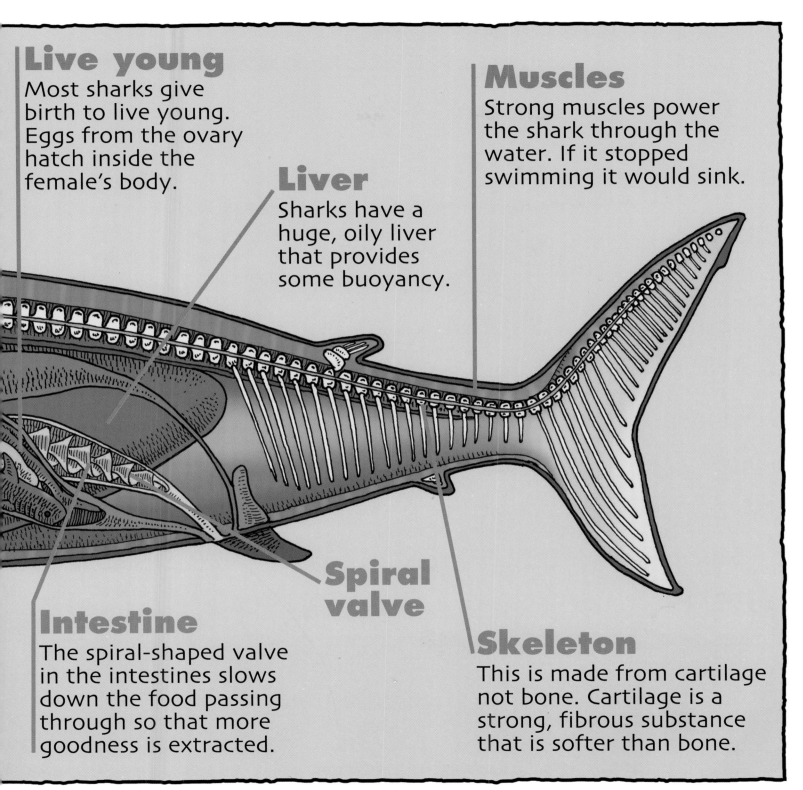

Live young

Most sharks give birth to live young. Eggs from the ovary hatch inside the female's body.

Liver

Sharks have a huge, oily liver that provides some buoyancy.

Muscles

Strong muscles power the shark through the water. If it stopped swimming it would sink.

Spiral valve

Intestine

The spiral-shaped valve in the intestines slows down the food passing through so that more goodness is extracted.

Skeleton

This is made from cartilage not bone. Cartilage is a strong, fibrous substance that is softer than bone.

Seahorse

Seahorses are fish that swim upright. They have a swim bladder and breathe through gills. They don't have scales. Their skin is stretched over an outside skeleton called an exoskeleton. They have long tails which they use to grasp weed or coral. They are good at camouflaging themselves to avoid **predators**. They can change colour very quickly to match their surroundings.

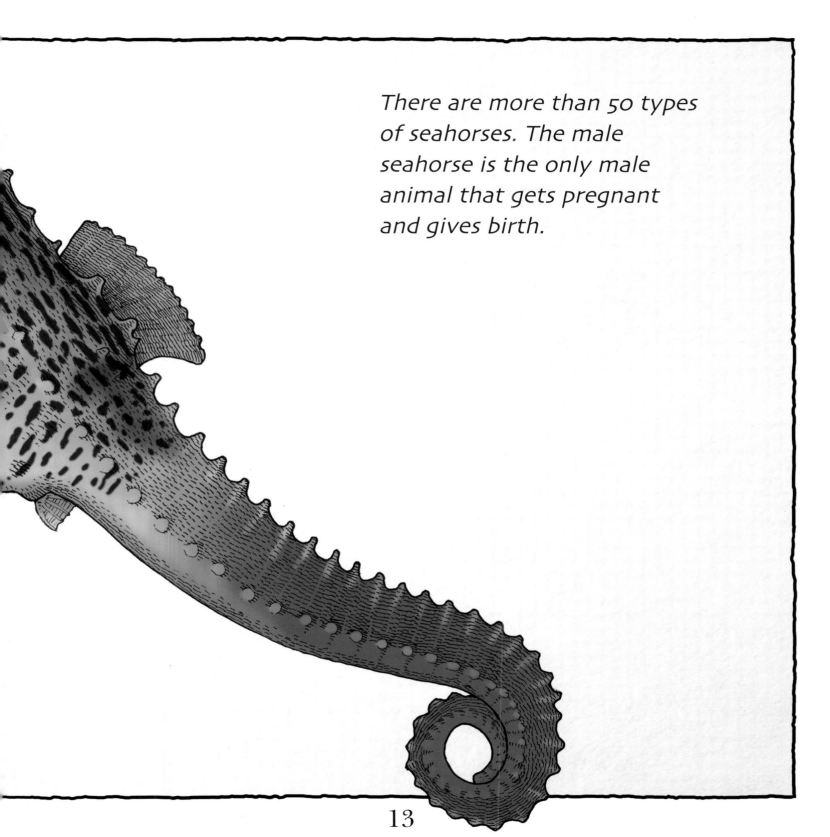

There are more than 50 types of seahorses. The male seahorse is the only male animal that gets pregnant and gives birth.

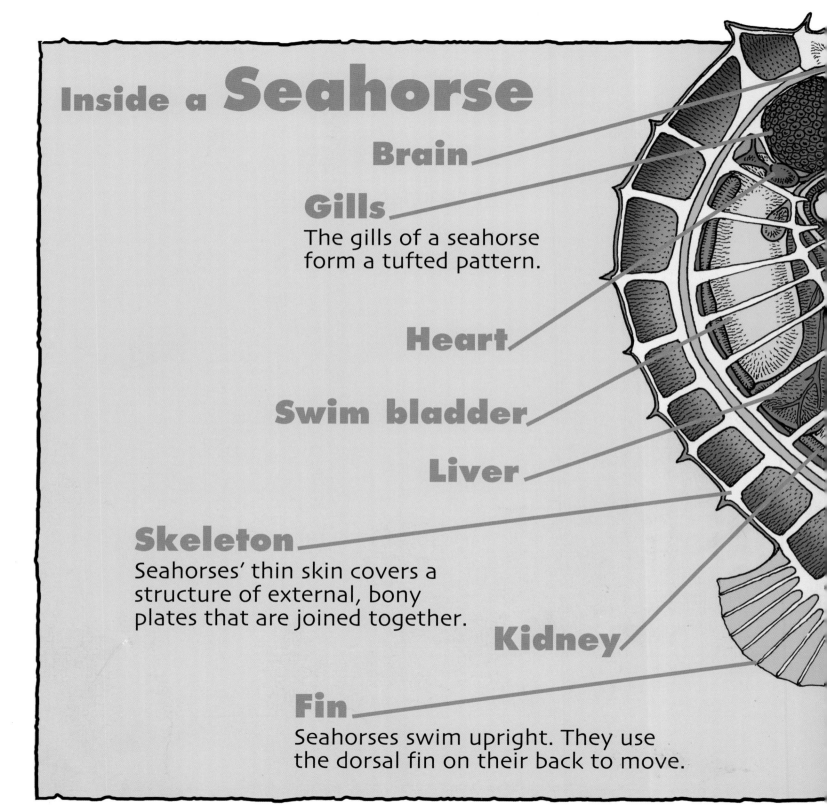

Inside a **Seahorse**

Brain

Gills

The gills of a seahorse form a tufted pattern.

Heart

Swim bladder

Liver

Skeleton

Seahorses' thin skin covers a structure of external, bony plates that are joined together.

Kidney

Fin

Seahorses swim upright. They use the dorsal fin on their back to move.

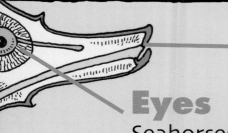

Snout
Seahorses use their long snouts to suck up food like a vacuum cleaner.

Eyes
Seahorses' eyes move independently of each other.

Intestines

Pouch
A female seahorse puts up to 1,500 eggs into the male's pouch. He then carries them for 9 to 45 days until the seahorses hatch and leave the pouch.

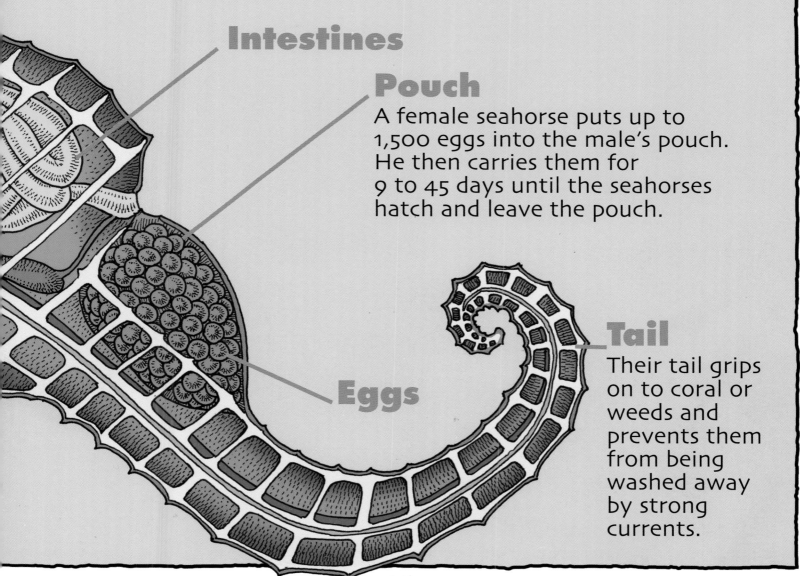

Eggs

Tail
Their tail grips on to coral or weeds and prevents them from being washed away by strong currents.

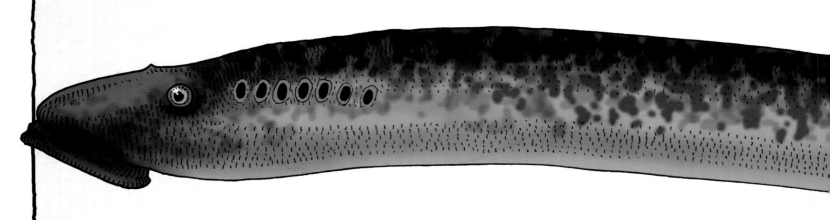

Lamprey

Lampreys are long, eel-like, jawless fish.
They have large eyes. Their head has one
nostril on the top and seven gill openings
on each side. They have a funnel-like,
sucking mouth with teeth. Some feed off
fish by latching on to their **prey** and
sucking their blood.

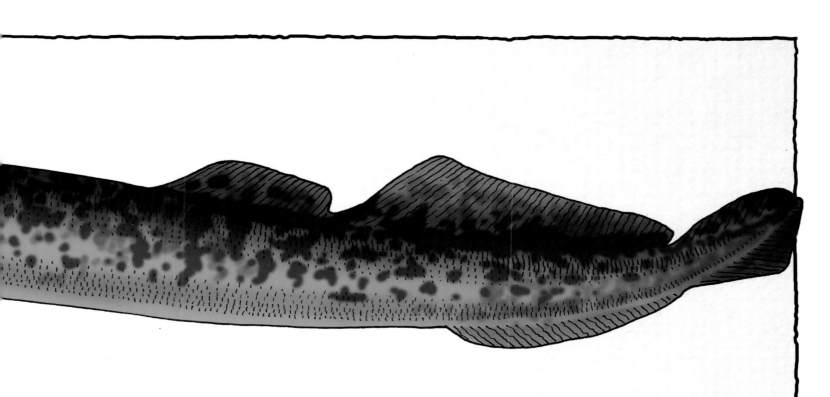

Most lampreys live in coastal and fresh
waters although some, like this sea
lamprey, travel long distances in the
ocean. They are born in rivers and travel
down river to the sea. They return to
the river to **spawn** before dying.

Inside a **Lamprey**

Nostril
Lampreys have a good sense of smell. They have only one nostril which is located on top of their head.

Brain

Heart

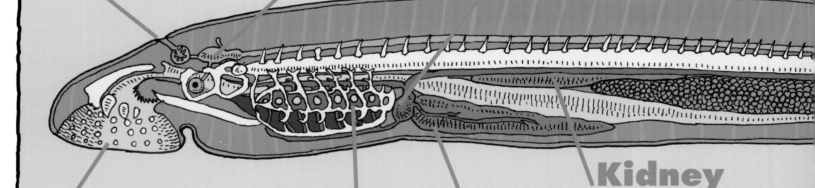

Kidney

Liver

Sucking mouth
Lampreys feed on prey by attaching their mouths to a fish's body. Their teeth cut through the skin and scales until they reach blood and body fluid.

Gills
Instead of water entering the mouth, it is pumped in and out of the seven gill holes on each side of the head.

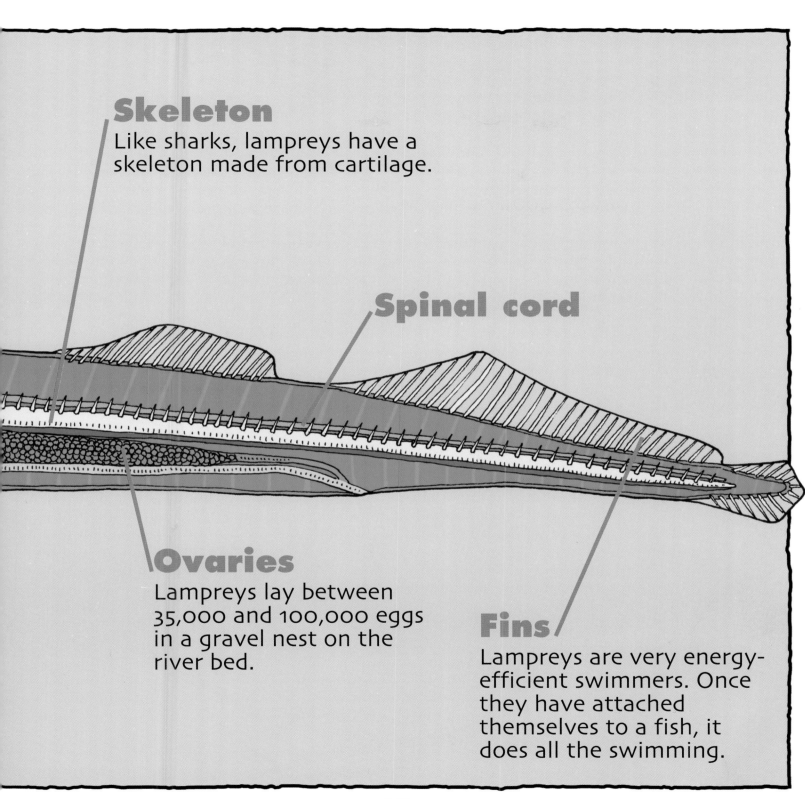

Skeleton
Like sharks, lampreys have a
skeleton made from cartilage.

Spinal cord

Ovaries
Lampreys lay between
35,000 and 100,000 eggs
in a gravel nest on the
river bed.

Fins
Lampreys are very energy-
efficient swimmers. Once
they have attached
themselves to a fish, it
does all the swimming.

Lungfish

Lungfish are freshwater fish that feed on fish, insects, crustaceans and plants. They are the only fish that can breathe air both out of water, using lungs, and underwater, using gills. Some lungfish can survive drought by burrowing into mud and hibernating until the rains return.

Lungfish like this marbled lungfish live in swamps, river beds, flood plains and river deltas in Africa. After the females spawn, males guard the nest of eggs from attack for about eight weeks.

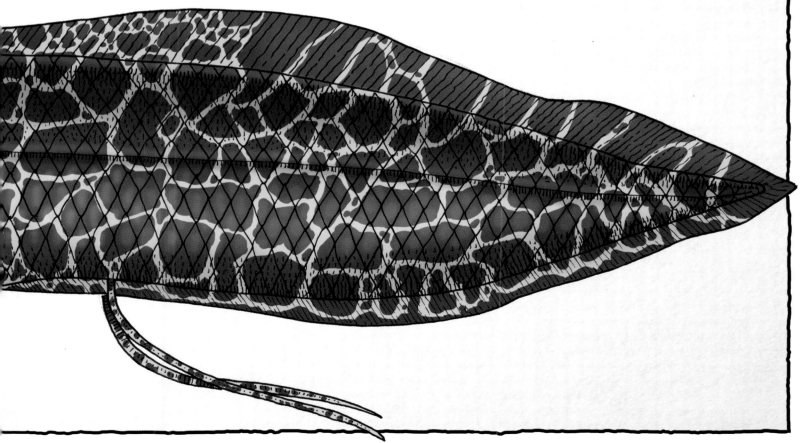

Inside a Lungfish

Spinal cord
This sends messages from the brain to the rest of the body.

Intestines

Brain

Gills
Lungfish use their gills to breathe when they are underwater.

Pectoral fins

Liver

Lungs
Lungfish can breathe air through a pair of lungs that are modified swim bladders.

Heart
The heart pumps blood through the lungs or gills to get oxygen.

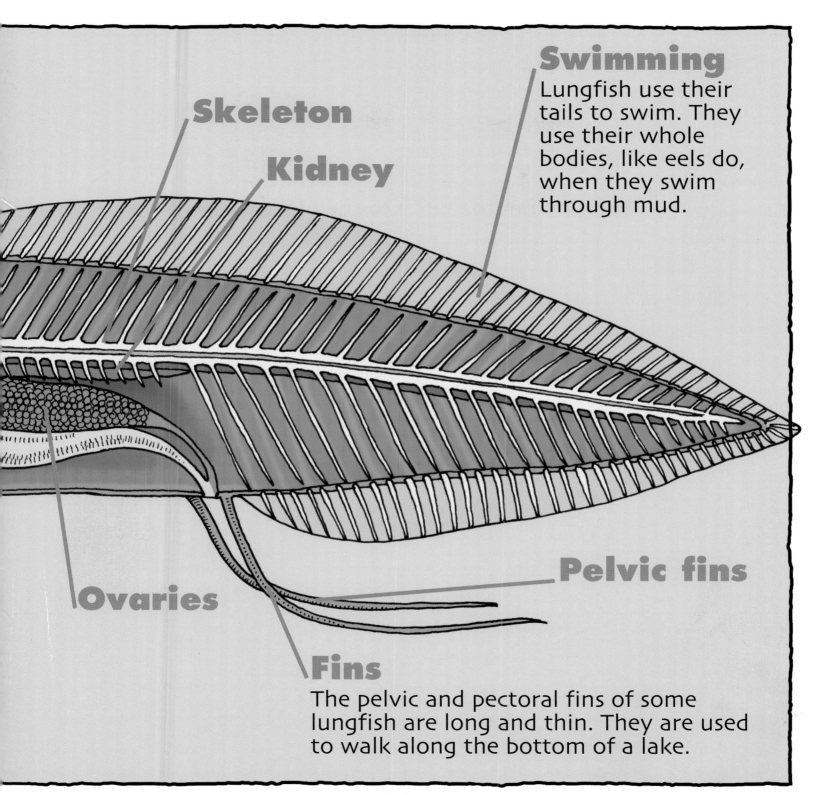

Skeleton

Kidney

Swimming
Lungfish use their tails to swim. They use their whole bodies, like eels do, when they swim through mud.

Ovaries

Pelvic fins

Fins
The pelvic and pectoral fins of some lungfish are long and thin. They are used to walk along the bottom of a lake.

Glossary

cartilage A strong, fibrous substance that is softer than bone.

crustacean A group of mainly water animals that includes crabs, lobsters and shrimps.

predator An animal that hunts and eats other animals.

prey An animal that is hunted and eaten by another animal.

scales Thin bony plates that cover and protect the skin of a fish or reptile.

spawn The release of, or laying of, eggs by a fish or amphibian.

Index

carp 5
cartilage 8, 11, 19
crustaceans 5, 20

denticles 10

eggs 4, 7, 11, 15, 19, 21
exoskeleton 13

fins 4, 6, 15, 19, 22, 23

gills 7, 10, 13, 14, 16, 18, 20, 22
great white 9

lakes 5, 23
lamprey 16–19
lungfish 20–23

ray-finned fish 4–7
rivers 5, 17, 19, 21

scales 4, 8, 13, 18
seahorse 12–15
shark 8–11
skeleton 4, 6, 8, 11, 13, 14, 15, 19, 23
swim bladder 7, 13, 14, 22

teeth 8, 10, 16, 18